The Big Red Dog Bakes a Cake

by Francie Alexander

Illustrated by Gita Lloyd and Eric Binder

SCHOLASTIC INC.

New York Toronto London Auckland Sydney
Mexico City New Delhi Hong Kong Buenos Aires

CAKE
JUMBO
CAKE
MIX

"Who will help me bake a cake?" asks Clifford The Big Red Dog.

"I will help bake the cake," says Cleo.

"I will help bake the cake," says T-Bone.

"I will help bake the cake," says K.C.

Jumbo CAKE mix
coconut flakes
Milk

“Who will help me make
the mix?” asks Clifford.

“I will,” says Cleo.
She gives him the milk.

“I will,” says T-Bone.
He gives him the
coconut flakes.

“I will,” says K.C.
He gives him the eggs.

To Emily
Elizabeth

"Who will help me take the cake?" asks Clifford.

"I will," says Cleo.
"Let me take the plates."

"I will," says T-Bone.
"Let's not be late."

"I will," says K.C.
"Let's race."

To Emily

The dogs take the cake.

The dogs race so they will not be late.

The cake shakes.

To Emily
Elizabeth

Oh, no!

The cake they made
falls down.

Cleo has a sad face.

T-Bone has a sad face.

K.C. has a sad face.

"Who will help me fix the
cake?" says Clifford.

They make many
small cupcakes.

They take the cupcakes
to the party.

They do not race to
Emily Elizabeth's place.

To Emily Elizabeth

"Who will help me taste the cupcakes?" asks Emily Elizabeth.

Cleo has a cupcake.

T-Bone does the same.

K.C. eats a cupcake.

Clifford The Big Red Dog does the same.

They eat and eat and eat.

Yum!